Contemporary Native Americans

MICHAEL DORRIS

BY
ANN WEIL

RSVP
RAINTREE
STECK-VAUGHN
P U B L I S H E R S
The Steck-Vaughn Company

Austin, Texas

Published by Raintree Steck-Vaughn, an imprint of Steck-Vaughn Company.
Produced by Mega-Books, Inc.
Design and Art Direction by Michaelis/Carpelis Design Associates.
Cover photo: ©Robert Maas/Sipa Press

Library of Congress Cataloging-in-Publication Data
Weil, Ann.
    Michael Dorris / by Ann Weil.
        p.   cm — (Contemporary Native Americans)
    Includes bibliographical references (p. 47) and index.
    Summary: Presents an overview of the life and work of this Native American author who has written works of fiction and nonfiction for both adults and children.
        ISBN 0-8172-3994-4 (Hardcover)
        ISBN 0-8172-6883-9 (Softcover)
    1. Dorris, Michael — Juvenile literature.   2. Authors, American — 20th century — Biography — Juvenile literature.   3. Indian authors — United States — Biography — Juvenile literature.   4. Indians of North America — Biography — Juvenile literature. 5. Indians in literature — Juvenile literature.   [1. Dorris, Michael.   2. Authors, American. 3. Indian authors.   4. Modoc Indians — Biography.   5. Indians of North America — Biography.]   I. Title.   II. Series.
PS3554.0695Z995   1997
813'.54 — dc21   96-44613
[B]   CIP
                                                                                    AC

Printed and bound in the United States.

1 2 3 4 5 6 7 8 9 LB 00 99 98 97 96

Contents

Chapter One

A NEW VOICE FOR NATIVE AMERICANS

In 1971 Michael Dorris sat in the waiting room of the Pierre, South Dakota, airport. He had his suitcase at his feet, and he carried a tiny stuffed animal tucked under one arm.

This was a big moment for Michael. He was 26 years old, single, and moments away from meeting the little boy he was hoping to adopt.

Suddenly the **social worker** from the South Dakota State Welfare Office greeted Michael and whisked him back to her office. A short time later, Michael met the boy for the first time. The toddler turned toward him. "Hi, Daddy," he said. In that instant Michael felt transformed—he had become a father.

Today it is not unusual for single men or women

Shining through the best-selling books of Michael Dorris is his fighting spirit. It is this spirit that helped him adopt Native American children as a single parent.

to adopt children. But in the early 1970s, many people considered women to be better parents than men. This idea was a stereotype—a kind of prejudice.

Michael Dorris fought against this stereotype of parenthood. He became one of the first men of our time to adopt a child as a single parent. But this was only the first of many stereotypes that Michael would fight against and win.

Michael Dorris is one of the best-known writers of Native American descent. He is part Modoc on his father's side. The Modoc is a small tribe who originally lived in northern California and southern Oregon. The tribe is known for refusing an order from the United States government to move to a **reservation**. The result was the Modoc War of 1872 and 1873. For a brief time after the war, the tribe moved to "Indian Territory," which is now known as Oklahoma. Today

Scarface Charley, a Modoc Indian who took part in the Modoc War (1872–1873). Michael's Native American ancestors come from the same tribe.

the majority of the Modoc live on reservations in the southern part of Oregon.

Michael's strong Modoc roots are one reason he is politically active in protecting the rights of Native Americans all over the United States. One issue he feels especially strong about is their right to live on reservations funded by the United States. Many people think that the government should not support reservations or give money to Native Americans. They don't understand that the money is not a handout—it is money the United States government owes the Native Americans for taking away their land many years ago.

Michael's first novel, *A Yellow Raft in Blue Water*, was published in 1987. This book became a best-seller. It tells the story of the lives of three Native American women. Michael's next book, *The Broken Cord*, was published in 1989 and became a best-seller, too. It also won the National Book Critics Circle Award that year. *The Broken Cord* is a nonfiction account, or true story, of Michael's discovery that his adopted son suffered special problems because his mother had drunk alcohol during her pregnancy. The book was later turned into a TV movie and watched by millions of people.

Michael has also written three books specifically for young readers. The first two, *Morning Girl* and *Guests*, are about young Native Americans and their first contact with the Europeans who arrived on their land.

Sees Behind Trees is about a young Powhatan boy who doesn't see well enough to hunt. The boy learns to use his other senses so well that the people in his village think he has magical powers.

One of Michael's goals has been to destroy the negative stereotypes of Native Americans. In the past many people have lumped all Native Americans together. They pictured them as red-skinned men clothed in buckskin with their faces painted with stripes of "war paint" and feathers sticking out from their long, straight, dark hair.

Michael is careful to portray the characters in his

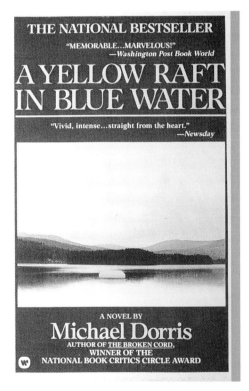

The cover of Michael's first best-selling novel. The story is told from the points of view of three different Native American women.

books as individuals. Readers everywhere—not just Native Americans—can identify with his characters and see the world through their eyes. Michael helps his readers discover that Native Americans have a unique culture, but they also have the same human strengths and weaknesses as everyone else.

Another stereotype that Dorris fights against has to do with the way a writer works. Many people think that writers come up with ideas all by themselves. Then they lock themselves in a room and work alone until the book is done. However, this is not the way Michael prefers to work.

Michael Dorris and his wife, author Louise Erdrich, are equal partners in their work. Michael and Louise plot their books together. Then every day they share whatever they've written on their own. Sometimes it is a few pages, other times it is only a paragraph. The book is not finished until they have agreed on every word.

Because Michael and Louise are well known for being Native American writers—Louise is also part Native American—many people assume that they speak for all Native Americans. But Michael feels that no one can speak for such a diverse group. Native Americans are one people, but they are also hundreds of different tribes. The tribes do not always share a common language or culture. So each tribe has its own story to tell.

Chapter Two

LOUISVILLE TO NEW HAMPSHIRE

Michael Anthony Dorris was born on January 30, 1945, in Louisville, Kentucky. His father, Jim Dorris, was a young army lieutenant. His mother, Mary Besy Burkhardt, met Jim on a blind date.

They were an attractive pair. Jim was a handsome "mixed-blood" man. Mary, who is part Irish, was a fun-loving woman with a big, beautiful smile. They married and spent their first years together living on army bases in Fort Lewis, Washington, and Brownwood, Texas.

When Mary became pregnant, she returned to her hometown of Louisville to live with her mother and her sister. A few months after Michael was born, his father left for Germany. That was the last time father and son were together. In 1947, when Michael was two years old, Jim Dorris was killed in a jeep accident in Germany.

It must have been a terribly sad time for Mary. She was now a widow and had very little money. Mary

Louisville, Kentucky, is the hometown of Michael's mother, Mary, and the city where he was born.

decided to stay in Louisville and live with her mother and sister. She was certain that among her mother, herself, and her sister, they could lavish enough love on Michael to soften the loss of his father.

Mary made sure that Michael's childhood was a full and happy one. They didn't have much money, but they did have a lot of fun. When she received free passes to the theater, she took Michael. When she won an all-expense-paid trip to Florida, she took him there, too. Every summer they went on a road trip with Michael's aunt Marion. They always made sure that they visited some of Michael's many relatives who lived scattered across the United States.

Michael's grandmother was a small, heavyset woman, with gray hair. But there was nothing small about her personality. Michael used to describe her as "queen of our house, demanding no less than total respect from the rest of the world."

Growing up with three strong, independent women had a definite influence on Michael's later life—both as a parent and as a writer. Michael learned that families did not have to be like the families in books and on TV, where "Dad" worked all day at an office and "Mom" baked all day in the kitchen. Michael learned that a family was a group of people who lived together and cared for each other.

The women in Michael's childhood had another

This 1948 photo shows Native American schoolchildren learning English. Next to the English words on the blackboard are the same words written in Navajo.

effect on him. When he began to write fiction, he realized that he could write just as well from a female point of view as from a male one. In fact his novels tend to have more female than male characters in them.

Another important influence on Michael had to do with his mixed blood. Michael was not raised on a reservation, but many of his summers were spent on reservations with his father's relatives.

Many Americans never experience more than one culture. Michael grew up in two cultures that are very different from one another—mainstream America in Louisville and Native America on reservations. Michael learned how to live in both.

One way Michael learned to live in both worlds was through reading books. Although Michael's mother, grandmother, and aunts lacked formal educations, they were very intelligent and well read. Michael grew up in a household that valued reading. So it was no accident that he became an avid reader as well as the first member of his family to get an education past grade school.

There was no bookstore in Michael's Louisville neighborhood—not that it really mattered, because his family didn't have money to buy books. Instead Michael went to the public library. His favorite books were from the "Little House" series by Laura Ingalls Wilder. In fact the first book he bought with his own money was *On the Banks of Plum Creek*, the fourth book in the series.

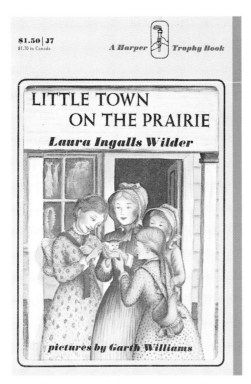

$1.50 | J7
$1.70 in Canada

A Harper **Trophy Book**

LITTLE TOWN
ON THE PRAIRIE
Laura Ingalls Wilder

pictures by Garth Williams

A cover of one of the "Little House" books in the classic series by Laura Ingalls Wilder. These books inspired Michael to learn more about his Native American culture.

The "Little House" books are about an early American family that travels west into "Indian country." Although he enjoyed these stories, young Michael quickly realized that the books often gave the wrong idea about or ignored Native Americans. Michael decided to learn more about his own Native American heritage. He spoke to elderly relatives about the past. He began to read history books and work on school projects about Native Americans.

Young Michael read other books in the children's section of his local library. He liked the Hardy Boys books a lot. But soon he wanted to read the books that were shelved on the other side of the checkout desk, in the adult section. When he was 11 years old, his aunt Marion gave him her library card and a note: "Please permit Michael to check out books for me." She did not say which books or how many he could take. This opened up a whole new world for Michael. He chose many different kinds of books to read— novels, history, and politics.

During the summer Michael mowed lawns to earn pocket money. One of his customers was an elderly man who sometimes paid Michael with books instead of cash. One of the books he gave Michael was titled *Coming of Age in Samoa*, by Margaret Mead, a famous anthropologist. An anthropologist studies the way people in different cultures live. In this book Ms. Mead wrote about the young people of Samoa, an island in the Pacific Ocean.

Michael never forgot *Coming of Age in Samoa* and ended up studying anthropology in college and graduate school. Many anthropologists do fieldwork, which means that they go to live with the people they are studying. Michael did his fieldwork in Alaska in 1971. He lived in a cabin in Tyonek, a Native American community on the west coast of Cook Inlet. There he collected information about how the modern world had changed the lives of people in that remote fishing village.

The native people in the village did not speak English. Michael spent a lot of time learning their language. One thing he learned was that they did not

Kackenack Bay in Homer, Alaska. While studying anthropology in 1971, Michael learned about the culture of the Tyoneks.

think of themselves as individuals. Instead of saying "I," they said "we" when speaking about themselves. Michael believed the Tyonek thought of themselves as a united group—like one large family.

The more time Michael spent with the Tyonek, the more he realized he wanted to have his own family, to become a "we," too. Michael began writing letters to adoption agencies. He worried about what the adoption agencies would say to a single man applying for a child. He knew that he wanted to marry someday, but there was no special woman in his life yet.

Sure enough many agencies wrote back saying they did not think a man could raise a child alone. But Michael was confident that he could do just that. After all, he had been raised in a single-parent home. In fact single parenthood was common in his family. His grandfathers and father had all died young. Their widows had raised the children alone with the help of other family members. They were strong, capable mothers, aunts, and grandmothers. He was certain that he could be a good single parent, too.

Other agencies said no to Michael because he did not make a lot of money. Michael wrote back explaining that he should not be disqualified because of a lack of money. He praised his own upbringing once again and the fact that his mother had done a fine job raising him on a small income.

Michael soon learned that adopting a child is a complicated process. First, one needs to be approved by a social service agency. The agency makes sure the person will be a good parent. Then the prospective parent waits until a child is available. Sometimes people wait for years.

Michael didn't say anything to his family about wanting to adopt. He was afraid that talking about adoption would jinx his chances. He continued his fieldwork and waited.

The only positive reply came from the nearby Alaska Catholic Social Services. Michael had to wait only a few months before he went for an interview. He dressed carefully in a dark suit and wore a tie for the first time in years. He told the nun who interviewed him that he was Native American and that he wanted to adopt a Native American baby. Despite his nervousness he knew that he had made a good impression. Even so, the nun told him not to get his hopes up.

But soon after the interview, Michael was approved. His name was forwarded to a national adoption agency that matched future parents to available children. Meanwhile, Michael accepted a new teaching job at Franconia College, in New Hampshire, and would be going there in late summer.

Michael started to think of himself as a father even before he had adopted his son. He rented a two-bedroom basement apartment and converted one of the bedrooms into a nursery. Soon he was ready. All he needed now was his baby.

Michael received the call from the adoption agency in early September 1971. There was a three-year-old Sioux boy available for adoption. Michael was at the agency's office a few hours later.

The social worker told Michael about the child. The boy had had a bad start on life. He was born premature—almost seven weeks earlier than he should have been. He had been neglected by his biological mother, who was an alcoholic. She had not fed him properly, and he suffered from malnutrition. When he was one year old, he became very ill with pneumonia, which is an infection of the lungs. He was taken away from his mother and placed in a foster home. Still his progress was not

Michael, as he looked while teaching at Dartmouth College. His area of study, as well as his pride in his heritage, can be seen in his choice of neckties.

good. He was small for his age, not toilet trained, and spoke only a few words.

The social worker probably thought that Michael would not be interested in adopting a little boy with so many problems. But he was wrong. Michael believed that with the proper care and love, his son would catch up. Michael's dream had come true.

Three

SINGLE FATHERHOOD

Michael organized his life around his son, whom he named Abel. They now lived in New Hampshire, and Michael was happier than he had ever been in his life. He loved Abel so much that it blinded him to what was obvious to almost everyone else. Abel had special problems, and they weren't getting any better.

One morning shortly after Abel's fourth birthday, something happened that made it impossible for Michael to deny his son's problems any longer. He had a seizure. Michael found Abel facedown on the floor, unconscious, and burning with a fever.

Michael rushed his son to the local hospital emergency room. The doctors there had no idea what was wrong with Abel. A friend advised Michael to take Abel to a bigger hospital, where Abel could get special care. Michael moved Abel to Dartmouth Medical Center, which was a half hour away in Hanover, New Hampshire. He hoped the doctors

Dartmouth Medical Center in Hanover, New Hampshire, where Michael took his son Abel for medical tests.

there could tell him what was wrong with his son.

During this crisis Michael was sure that once his son's illness was identified, it could be treated. Then they could continue with their lives. But the doctors at Dartmouth Medical Center didn't know what was wrong with Abel either.

Medical tests showed that Abel had a number of problems. Some had to do with his brain, others with his spine, and still more problems with his joints. The doctors were stumped—they knew of no disease that caused all of these symptoms. They kept the boy in the hospital for a week.

One afternoon Michael was reading to his son, when two young Native American men entered the room. They explained that they were students at

Dartmouth College and had heard of Michael and of his son's illness. The young men explained to Michael that Dartmouth was originally founded as a school for Native Americans, but over the years, that focus had been lost. Now Dartmouth was beginning a Native American Studies program. The college hoped to attract more Native American students and educate all students about Native American culture. These two young men wanted to know if Michael was interested in directing the program.

Michael was definitely interested! He missed the

Michael teaching at Dartmouth College in 1975. Michael was the Director of the Native American Studies program, as well as a teacher of anthropology.

company of other Native Americans. There was a common bond among Native Americans—even those of different tribes. Also Abel was a full-blooded Sioux child, and it was important to Michael for his son to grow up around other Native Americans.

Three weeks after Abel left the hospital, he had another seizure. Abel's small body jerked uncontrollably. Saliva dribbled from his mouth. His eyes rolled up in his head. Michael hadn't witnessed the first seizure that had sent Abel to the hospital. Michael was pained by such a violent and upsetting attack on his young son. Worst of all Michael was helpless to prevent Abel's seizures.

Abel went back to the hospital. After many more tests, the doctors were still stumped. Abel took medicine to control the seizures while Michael hoped for the best. However, Abel continued to fall further behind the other children in his day-care group. He could not identify his crayons by color. He could not even count to five. Still unwilling to face the fact that his son was "not normal," Michael did his best to help Abel and secretly blamed the medicine.

In 1972 Dartmouth offered Michael a teaching job. They wanted him to teach anthropology and also to start the Native American Studies program. He accepted. It was perfect—he would be teaching a subject he felt passionate about, and Abel would be closer to the doctors at the medical center.

Michael rented a cabin on a nearby lake. He enrolled Abel in day care. Michael thought that this would be a new start for both of them. But Abel still did not make progress. He was still in diapers and obviously behind the other children.

Despite these frustrations Michael and Abel had fun together. Michael was as devoted to his son as his own mother had been to him. It was a very busy time for Michael. Through Michael's hard work, the Native American Studies program got off the ground. It attracted Native American students and teachers from all over the country. Soon there was a small Native American community at Dartmouth.

One of Michael's new friends was a Standing Rock Lakota anthropologist. *Lakota* means "the people" in the Sioux language. The anthropologist, Beatrice Medicine, invited Michael and Abel to visit her mother's house on the Standing Rock reservation. Standing Rock is located in South Dakota. It is part of what remains of the Great Sioux Reservation that the United States government created in 1868. There was going to be a large celebration while they were there, and Abel would receive a Lakota name.

Michael was thrilled with the invitation. He wanted Abel to feel at home with people who shared his Sioux heritage. His son would be getting a Lakota name—a sign of acceptance. Michael let Abel's hair grow long enough for the traditional Lakota braids. He let his own hair grow, too. A friend had made them both special shirts for the ceremony.

When they began their trip, and as they got closer

A Sioux Indian in ceremonial dress. Michael and his son, Abel, who was a full-blooded Sioux, were given Lakota names during a 1973 ceremony.

to the reservation, Michael became more and more nervous. Michael had spent a lot of time earlier on reservations and had sometimes felt like an outsider. More than anything he wanted to be accepted by his son's people. When they arrived Michael was excited to find out that he would receive a Lakota name, too.

The ceremony was beautiful. Since Michael didn't understand the Lakota language, Beatrice Medicine translated for him. Michael watched proudly as his son was called forward to receive his name. Abel's Lakota name was Wood Mountain.

Then it was Michael's turn. He walked up and

stood next to his son. His Lakota name was Eagle Wing, and he was presented with a large, beautiful headdress of eagle feathers.

Michael was stunned. The headdress was the ultimate symbol of belonging. Michael realized that without Abel he would never have been part of the glorious ceremony, and his bond with his son grew even stronger.

Michael enjoyed his job at Dartmouth College. But being a single parent, especially the parent of a child with special needs, left little time for dating. Michael began to feel as if he might not marry. Yet he wanted a bigger family.

This photo shows Dartmouth Hall in Dartmouth, New Hampshire. Michael's work at the college, in addition to being a single parent, kept him very busy.

In 1974 Michael adopted a two-year-old boy. He named his second son Jeffrey Sava, after a good friend he knew from his days in Alaska. Like six-year-old Abel, Jeffrey Sava was a full-blooded Sioux child from South Dakota.

Abel was thrilled to have a brother. Michael was startled by Sava's development. He was toilet trained in two months. He learned how to tie his shoes—something Abel was still struggling with. Now that Michael could compare Abel to Sava, there was no way of denying the truth. Abel's problems were not going to go away.

Michael adopted a third child, a ten-month-old girl, in 1976. He named her Madeline Hannah. Like her brothers, Madeline was also a full-blooded Sioux from South Dakota.

This was a happy time for Michael, but it wasn't always easy. He was busy with work and caring for his children, especially Abel. They lived in a large old farmhouse he had bought for very little money. Michael was promoted from assistant professor to associate professor.

Abel attended grade school in Cornish, New Hampshire. He was a loving, trusting boy, and his teachers adored him. Although Abel made progress at school, it was very slow.

In 1979 Michael and his family attended the Dartmouth Powwow. The Powwow is a big party Dartmouth has thrown every year since 1973. There was dancing, and traditional Native American foods were served. Many of Michael's former students were there, including Karen Louise Erdrich.

Michael had first met her in 1972. It was natural that the two became friends. They had similar backgrounds. Both were part Native American. Karen was a member of the Turtle Mountain Band of Chippewa. Both were raised Catholic. Still, he was a professor, and she was his student. They were friends, nothing more.

The two kept in touch after Karen left Dartmouth. They spoke on the phone occasionally and sent each other Christmas cards. Michael learned that after graduation Karen had become a traveling poetry teacher in North Dakota. She also worked on a Nebraska Public Television film about Native Americans. Karen received a master's degree at the Writing Workshop of Johns Hopkins University. By 1979 she lived in Boston and was editing *The Circle,* the Boston Indian Council newspaper. Most exciting of all, her poems had been published in several magazines.

By the time of the Powwow, Michael had not seen Karen for four years. She had dropped her first name, Karen, and went by Louise Erdrich. Michael had known Louise as a bright student. Now he was struck by her grace and beauty as well.

A few weeks later, Michael attended a poetry reading Louise gave at Dartmouth. He listened, transfixed, as she read her work. It was then that he

A Dartmouth Powwow, a tradition at the school since 1973. It was during one of these Powwows that Michael's friendship with former student Louise Erdrich began to grow deeper.

realized he was in love with her. Later that evening, as he drove her to the house where she was staying, Michael had an overwhelming urge to propose marriage right then and there.

Michael didn't know it at the time, but Louise felt the same way about him. That same night she called her mother to say she had met the man she was going to marry.

LOUISE ERDRICH: WIFE AND PARTNER

There was no time for Michael to pursue a romance with Louise. A week after the poetry reading, he and his children were on their way to New Zealand for nine months. Michael had won a **research fellowship** and was going to study the native people of New Zealand, a large island group near Australia.

Michael's first task was to enroll his children in school. He found a special education program for Abel. Sava and Madeline made new friends easily, but Abel kept pretty much to himself as he had in New Hampshire. By this time Abel was 12 years old. He had completed seven years of school. Most of that time he was in special learning programs, but he still lacked basic skills.

The months in New Zealand passed quickly for Michael. He and Louise wrote to each other often.

With writer Louise Erdrich, Michael found his fairest critic, as well as his most powerful inspiration.

After years of writing only **academic papers** and books, Michael began to write **fiction**. He sent some of his poems and short stories to Louise. She sent him poems and stories of her own. They focused on each other's work, carefully avoiding the subject of their own relationship—a friendship that might become something more.

In New Zealand, Michael had the time and inspiration to write more fiction. A lot of that inspiration came from Louise. She was totally honest about his work, as he was about hers. Michael quickly realized that every criticism she gave him was exactly the right suggestion.

Louise and Michael are partners in their careers as well as in marriage. They share a similar background and a mutual respect.

Before long it was time for Michael and the children to return to New Hampshire. The day after they arrived home, they went to the airport to meet Louise's flight. She was coming back to Dartmouth as part of the Native American Studies **writer-in-residence** program. During this time Michael and Louise continued to share their work with each other. They spent many hours together discussing their writing. As the months passed, their relationship became romantic.

Michael and Louise were married in October 1981, in a ceremony that included Michael's three children. A year later Louise adopted the children as well. Now they shared the responsibilities of raising a family as they continued to work together.

Their first **collaborations** were short stories they sold to magazines. They published the stories using a pen name, Milou North. Milou was a combination of the first few letters of their first names. They chose North as the last name because New Hampshire is one of the most northern states. One of their Milou North stories appeared in *Redbook* magazine. The rest were published in England.

One day Michael received a note from one of his relatives. It was about a short-story contest with a $5,000 prize. When he told Louise about the contest, she didn't want to enter. The deadline was less than two weeks away. It was school vacation, so the children were home. They had houseguests staying in her study, so she didn't have a quiet place to work. But Michael thought they could do it and convinced her to try.

Louise sat at the kitchen table and wrote throughout the day. She started with an idea about a family reunion. Meanwhile, Michael sprained his back. He was in terrible pain. He lay flat on the floor. Louise brought parts of her story to him. He held them up in front of his face to read.

It wasn't the ideal way to work, but they finished their story and sent it in just in time. Although they both worked on the story, they submitted it under Louise's name. She had had the idea for the story, and she had written the first draft.

While they waited for the results, Michael and

Louise thought about everything they would change in the story. They were as surprised as anyone when they found out that they had won. The judges chose Louise's short story, "The World's Greatest Fisherman," from among 2,000 entries.

Winning *Chicago Magazine*'s 1982 Nelson Algren Award for fiction was a turning point in their lives. They not only received the $5,000, but they were also finally convinced that they had what it took to be successful writers.

A portrait of Michael taken in 1989. By this time he had become a teacher, a husband, and a successful author.

Chapter Five

ALCOHOL AND PREGNANCY DON'T MIX

"The World's Greatest Fisherman" became the first chapter of Louise's novel *Love Medicine*, published in 1984. *Love Medicine* tells the story of Native Americans who live on a reservation. The novel is made up of many chapters, each one a short story in itself. At first Louise had the chapters in a totally different order. Michael thought the chapters would work better another way. They argued about it night after night. Finally he convinced her to try it his way.

This restructuring of the novel was only one of Michael's significant contributions to *Love Medicine*. Part of the time, Michael and Louise worked on the novel separately. Other times they worked together at a big table in the living room of their New Hampshire house. They spread out the pages Louise had written and discussed the novel thoroughly.

They got to know the characters in the book as if they were real people with real lives. They would talk about them during long evening walks. When they went out to eat in a restaurant, they imagined what their characters would order from the menu. When they looked through a clothing catalog, they would discuss what the characters would wear. Michael and Louise had fun getting to know their characters, but collaborating was not always easy. Sometimes they each had different ideas about the way the story worked best. They would argue over a word or a sentence. Sometimes they traded—"I'll get rid of this line, if you will get rid of that line."

Love Medicine was the first novel Michael and Louise worked on together. It became an award-winning best-seller.

Love Medicine was the first of many projects that were published with only one of their names as the author. Louise and Michael felt that when people read a book, they liked it to be by only one person. Michael never had any problem with that. He didn't mind that his name was not on every book cover.

When their agent was not successful in getting *Love Medicine* published, Michael stepped in. He became Louise's agent. He had stationery printed that said The Michael Dorris Agency. Michael refused to give up. Before he found a publisher for the book, he sold chapters of the book to magazines.

Love Medicine became a best-seller with rave reviews. It also won many awards, including the National Book Critics Circle best work of fiction of 1984. It was an exciting time for Michael and Louise. Louise had another book published in 1984. This time it was a collection of her poetry called *Jacklight*.

But success did not really change their lives. They were still as busy as ever. Their family grew. Eventually Louise and Michael had three daughters in addition to the children they had adopted. Their home life was hectic. They were either up all night with a baby or involved in a crisis with Abel or one of the other older children.

Michael had no problem remaining in the background while his wife became a successful published author. He knew that her success was his as well. And he was working on projects of his own. One of them was a nonfiction book that he titled *The Broken Cord*.

The Broken Cord is about Michael's realization that Abel's birth defects were caused by his mother's drinking while she was pregnant. It took Michael six years to finish the book. His discovery began in 1982, when Michael visited a drug treatment center for teens on a South Dakota reservation. The young boys he saw there looked and acted exactly like Abel.

Michael felt that this had to be more than a coincidence. Michael took a photo of Abel from his wallet and showed it to the director of the treatment center. The director examined the picture. He told Michael that Abel had FAS, Fetal Alcohol Syndrome. As Michael listened to the man explain the symptoms, he realized it was the first time he had ever heard of FAS.

Michael thought back to when Abel had been a baby and how he had hoped the doctors could diagnose his son's problems—and teach Michael how to help Abel. This never happened. Now, ten years later, Michael found the cause of Abel's problems. But the sad truth was there was still nothing Michael could do to help. FAS is irreversible. Once the damage has been done, it cannot be undone.

Michael spent many of the following years researching Fetal Alcohol Syndrome. FAS is a problem all over the world. There are no exact figures for children born with FAS or a milder form, called Fetal Alcohol Effect (FAE). It is impossible to tell at birth which children are affected. The symptoms of

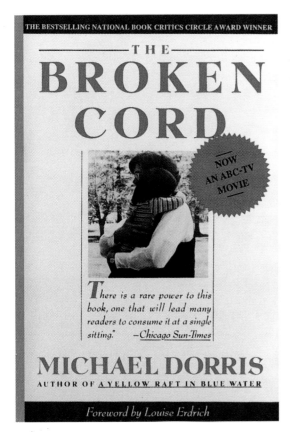

Michael's labor of love, *The Broken Cord*, introduced the problem of Fetal Alcohol Syndrome to many people.

FAS and FAE appear as the children develop. Most children are never formally diagnosed at all.

The only solution is to teach mothers not to drink while they're pregnant. *The Broken Cord* educated many people to the dangers of drinking during pregnancy. Michael gave hundreds of interviews and appeared on many television talk shows. He wanted to get the message to as many people as possible. And he succeeded. In 1990, partly due to Michael's efforts in making the public more aware of FAS, a federal law was passed. The law required every beer, wine, and

The success of *The Broken Cord* made it possible for the book to be made into a TV movie, starring Jimmy Smits. Like the book, the movie touched millions of people and won many awards.

liquor bottle to have a label warning people of the risks of drinking alcohol during pregnancy.

The Broken Cord was published in 1989. More than his other books, this was a family project. Abel wrote his own version of his life story. It is included in the book as well. Michael and Louise knew that by publishing *The Broken Cord*, they were putting themselves and their family on display. They are very private people, but they gave up their privacy in the hope that their story might just stop someone, somewhere, from producing a child with FAS.

The Broken Cord was such a successful book that Hollywood producers decided to make it into a TV movie. In 1991 Michael went to California to discuss the production with famous actors and directors. But the day he arrived, he received word that Abel had been hit by a car. The driver had not seen him as Abel crossed a street at night.

It was an accident from which Abel would not recover.

Chapter Six

A NEW PERSPECTIVE ON AMERICA

Losing a child is a parent's worst nightmare. It is unbelievably painful. Michael and his family needed time to accept Abel's death. They followed a tribal tradition and waited a year before holding a small memorial service. They chose a spot above the pond near their house that Abel had loved. They planted a strong, young maple tree as his marker. After the simple ceremony, they stood by the tree in silence for a long time. They told stories about Abel and laughed and cried. Finally each family member and friend said good-bye to Abel.

Meanwhile, filming of *The Broken Cord* continued. Michael's first impulse was to walk away from the project. He didn't want to think about Abel's death anymore. But he realized that the movie was a way for Abel to help people even after his death. Michael

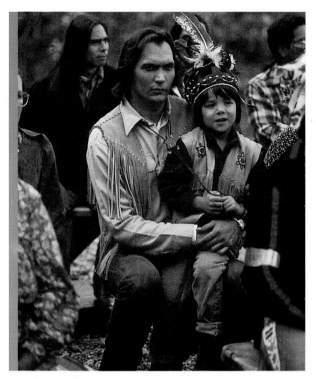

Jimmy Smits and Frederick Lederer in a scene from *The Broken Cord*. In real life Abel's tragic death during the making of the film made the movie's message even more important and powerful.

knew that the movie would bring a powerful meaning to Abel's short life and tragic death.

Like the book, the movie version of *The Broken Cord* won many awards. More importantly though, it accomplished Michael's goal. Over 30 million people watched the movie.

Michael himself never watched the movie. He has his own memories of his son to cherish.

While Michael is probably best known for *The Broken Cord,* he is gaining recognition for his works of fiction for both adults and young readers. Many of the characters in his stories and novels are young people searching for a sense of their own identities.

The novel *The Crown of Columbus* carried both Michael's and Louise's names. The research for the book inspired one of Michael's books for young adults, *Morning Girl*.

Sometimes this feeling of not belonging has to do with a character's ethnic identity. Michael denies that his books are autobiographical, or based on his own life. Still there are strong similarities between his own feelings of insecurity and those of his characters.

The character Rayona in the book *A Yellow Raft in Blue Water* is part Native American, and part African American. When she and her mother move to a reservation, 15-year-old Rayona feels like an outsider. It doesn't help when her full-blooded Native American cousin teases her about her dark skin. Rayona's big moment comes when she substitutes for her cousin at a rodeo—something Michael did when he was a teenager. Like Michael, Rayona gets thrown off the same horse three times.

Many of Michael's books and stories focus on family relationships. This is one of the themes of *Morning Girl*. It was his first book for young readers, and it was published in 1992. The characters Morning Girl and her brother Star Boy are young Native Americans who live on a tropical island. At the end of the story, Morning Girl sees a canoe filled with men wearing strange clothes, heading for shore. One of the men is Christopher Columbus.

Michael got the idea for *Morning Girl* when he and Louise were researching another novel, *The Crown of Columbus*. Part love story, part mystery, and part adventure, the novel is about two college professors who are researching the life of Columbus.

Michael's second book for young readers, titled *Guests*, was published in 1994. *Guests* is about a Native American boy named Moss. He is angry that his father has invited a bunch of strangers to share their special harvest meal. Just as *Morning Girl* gives readers a different perspective on Columbus "discovering" America, *Guests* gives another perspective about the first Thanksgiving.

Michael's books have given many people a new point of view about both America and American people. It is an appropriate legacy for a descendent of the original Americans.

Important Dates

1945   Born in Louisville, Kentucky, on January 30.

1947   Michael's father, Jim Dorris, killed in World War II.

1971   Michael begins studying the Tyonek Native American Community and adopts his first child, a full-blooded Sioux boy he names Abel.

1972   Michael accepts teaching job at Dartmouth College.

1974   Michael adopts another full-blooded Sioux boy he names Jeffrey Sava.

1976   Michael adopts a full-blooded Sioux girl and names her Madeline Hannah.

1981   Marries Louise Erdrich.

1982   Michael and Louise win the Nelson Algren Award for their short story, "The World's Greatest Fisherman." Michael discovers Abel has Fetal Alcohol Syndrome (FAS).

1984   Michael's first joint novel with Louise, *Love Medicine*, is published and becomes a best-seller.

1987   *A Yellow Raft in Blue Water* is published.

1989   *The Broken Cord* is published and wins the National Book Critics Circle Award.

1991   *The Broken Cord* is made into a TV movie. Before the movie is completed, Abel dies in a tragic accident.

Glossary

academic papers   Research papers that are written for a school assignment.

collaboration   A project that two or more persons work on together.

fiction   Written works that tell about made-up characters or events.

research fellowship   Money given to students to help them live while they continue their studies.

reservation   An area of land set aside by the United States government for Native Americans to live on.

social worker   A person who provides aid to people who are in need of clothing or shelter.

writer-in-residence   A published writer who has been invited to live at a university while teaching classes to students.

Bibliography

Dorris, Michael. *Native Americans: Five Hundred Years After.* Photography by Joseph C. Farber. Crowell, 1977.

Dorris, Michael. *Morning Girl.* Hyperion, 1992.

Dorris, Michael. *Guests.* Hyperion, 1995.

Index